creating a leader

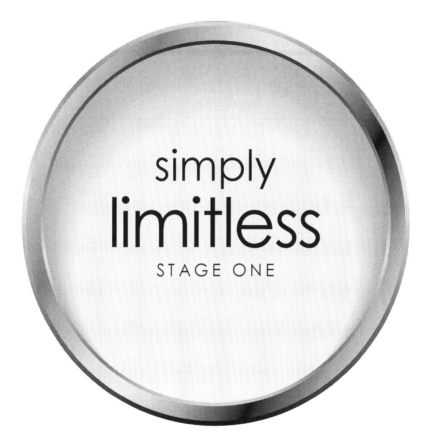

simply
limitless
STAGE ONE

creating a leader

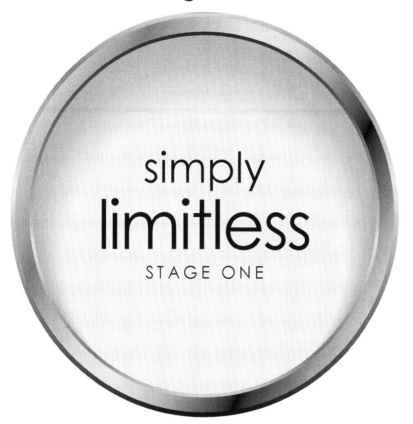

simply
limitless
STAGE ONE

Kelly A. McCormack

Wayland, Massachusetts

Creating a Leader Publishing Division
P. O. Box 5164
Wayland, MA 01778
www.creatingaleader.com

Printed in the United States of America
First Printing, 2017
ISBN 978-1-945943-00-3

The information contained within this book is strictly my opinion from my personal experiences. This book is not intended to be a substitute for the medical advice of a licensed physician. Readers should consult with their doctor in any matters relating to his/her health. If you wish to apply any of the ideas contained in this book, you accept full responsibility for your actions. This includes any support that you may need if you have adverse reactions to reading this material.

The Leadership Score™, FutureCam™ and Creating a Leader™ are trademarks of Creating a Leader.

Edited by Leslie Conner
Cover and interior design by Desktop Miracles
Illustrations by Kelly McCormack

dedication and acknowledgement

This book is written for you, the leader who is courageous enough to see that we can create a better world around us.

I acknowledge you for stepping onto this path and taking a journey into the best, most creative and impactful version of yourself.

I give you my respect, compassion, and hard-fought learning within these pages. It is my deepest hope that they will help to make the steps of your path lighter.

Enjoy the journey!

contents

Hi! I'm Kelly.
This is the
Path to Creating
Limitlessly as a Leader.
We'll take it step-by-step.
This book is for everyone and
nobody will get left behind!

We will even get to
have some fun along the way
with exercises and Story Time.
Hope you enjoy the journey!

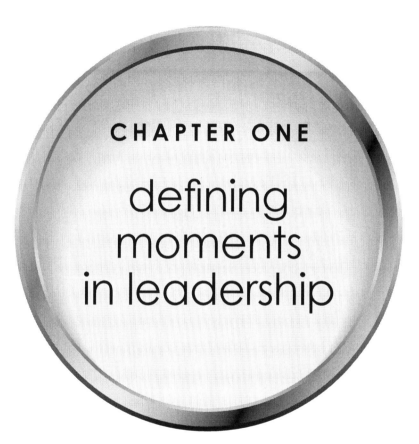

CHAPTER ONE

defining
moments
in leadership

Our world needs leaders now.

This book series presents the 7.5 billion people on Earth a pathway to step into and grow in leadership.

Leadership is our innate right. Defined well, it can bring us to a brand-new world that honors every individual while leaving space for each of us to intelligently envision a beautiful future, invite others to join in, and to realize those visions together.

Leadership

Power

Create

Unconscious

What's in a word?

Vision

Execute

Empower

Develop

Yet, if we are to find ourselves within a reality that is worth living, somehow we would have to fully understand what our role is in bringing that about. And to do so requires that we go down to...

the smallest single unit of communication —the word—

...to find out how it holds the key to the empowerment of every person on earth.

why do definitions matter?

Similar to how a specific currency has become the trusted medium of exchange that allows us to buy and sell our goods and services, all cultures have an agreement about the medium of the word and how that allows us to exchange meaning with one another.

Take, for example, the word **labor.**

To a pregnant mother, this will be the start of a whole new journey. To a worker, this will be something done in exchange for money. For the owner of a business, this will be one of the critical inputs — along with vision, a process, raw material, and so on — that produce a product. While in Britain, this will represent a specific viewpoint in politics. This word is the same word. In some cases, it could have the exact same intended meaning, yet it holds different connotations for everybody involved.

In addition to different meanings for the same word, some words have shifted their meaning over time, based on events of cultural progression and regression. While we still use the word as a medium of exchange of ideas, we must recognize that this medium *can* contain old baggage.

What if . . .

What would your life be like if the definitions of words changed randomly and you didn't know it?

When a word is not clearly defined, it is subject to the bias and interpretation of all of the users of that word. In the case of the word "leadership," which is woven into the fabric of our society, time has worn away the clarity and effectiveness of its meaning. "Leadership," when defined well, CAN support and serve everyone's ability to *create without limits*. In order to solidify the foundation of society, we may choose to proactively clarify the meaning.

This is literally a redefining moment in humanity.

defining leadership

Defining leadership is very simple, which is what gives it its power. If we take the word management out of the picture, a leader is simply somebody who brings something, anything into being.

Leadership is
THE POWER TO CREATE.

Have you had a tea with a friend?

Leader

Have you parented a child?

Leader

Have you exchanged with someone in a way that brought value to both of you?

Leader

Have you helped your community somehow?

Leader

Have you run a business or worked in a business?

Leader

Have you made your breakfast, comforted a friend, or climbed up a mountain?

Leader, Leader, Leader!

When we settle for only using the word in businesses, government, and communities, we lose the power that is available to all to create at greater and greater levels. Let's take a look into the parts of the definition to see what makes up a leader.

the definition of power

Leadership is often associated with power. The use of *leadership* along with *power* has migrated into the implied use of the word "over" (i.e. power over). We can see this in the way that leadership and power are being used as words of superiority. It wasn't always this way.

If we go all the way back to where the word power comes from, we see it was Latin and means "be able" — not to *be over*, but simply to *be able*. To *be able* implies that the ability or potential is there to create something. Power drives creation. When we couple that with the definition of create, we begin to see how simply each one of us will find an ability to powerfully express ourselves through the visions we hold dearly.

the definition of create

Create means to bring something into existence.

Something doesn't exist, a leader envisions a new way of looking at the circumstance, executes on that vision, and now it exists. This could be in the form of a relationship experience, a business improvement, or bringing a smile to someone's face.

The Visionary Zone . . .

. . . if this was your bubble, what vision would you create inside of it?

"It seems too simple . . ."

*The Power to Create begins
with an understanding that
it takes **Power** to Create.*

leadership as the power to create

When we bring this all together, we can see how we have **defined leadership**.

Power

means

be able

to Create

means

to bring something into existence

And we shorthand the definition as

The Power to Create.

TOM'S HARDWARE STORE

As we saw earlier, the definition of leadership and power have regressed in many parts of humanity. Leadership and power over, with "over" being implied, is part of the reason this could happen.

So how do cultures "agree" upon the changes in definitions over time? To begin to answer that, we will look at the neuroscience and psychology of a leader, which will enable you to...

...fill your leadership tool box with basic tools and their definitions.

defining
the conscious mind

The conscious mind is the part of our mind where we can recall information, support some life-sustaining processes, and **create** new possibilities. Many humans think their mind operates in a pretty conscious manner, but this is very far from the truth. The conscious mind represents only about 1 to 5% of our process. For this reason, the iceberg is often used as a metaphor. You can see the tip of the iceberg, while a far greater amount of ice is sitting below the surface, below what we can see.

the (sub) unconscious mind

The unconscious (to us) mind operates **based on our past programming**. The subconscious mind has significantly greater capacity for processing than that of the conscious mind. When there is a war of will between the subconscious and the conscious mind, the subconscious mind has thousands of times more power over what the conscious mind is trying to create.

In order to become better, more conscious leaders, we will want to explore the elements of unconsciousness. That's where we will go next . . .

CHAPTER TWO

the unconscious human processor

The preciousness of life seeps in through the openness we create.

Since the greatest majority of processing is done below the conscious level of the mind, exploring the unconscious portion of the mind is critical to increase the power which helps us to create. If we were to understand how we become unconscious, then we could begin to turn that into being more conscious.

This consciousness is directly translated into power.

Let's look at the story of how our human processing works.

programming and unconsciousness

As you sit reading this book, take a look around at your current environment.

Take everything in that you possibly can.

First, what do you **smell**?
What subtle scents come through?

What do you **hear**?
Perhaps there is a bird sound in the distance. Perhaps the buzz of a refrigerator. Maybe the ticking of a clock.

How about what you **see**?
Are there patterns and shapes in the room? What are the colors?

What do you **taste**?
Perhaps you just finished a tea or coffee and still have that taste in your mouth.

What do you **feel** on your skin?
Is there a coolness or a warmth? Do you feel any tingling or sense of aliveness in your skin?

In addition to these five senses that are traditionally thought of as external, what internal senses and processing are you experiencing?

Do you have **thoughts** that are conscious to you?
Do you recognize any of the thoughts that exist underneath your consciousness that may be presenting themselves in the form of questions like, "Where is this book going?"

What are you **feeling** inside?

What **emotions** are you experiencing?

What **beliefs** are operating for you in this very moment? For example, do you believe it is easy to read this book or difficult to read this book? Do you believe it's possible for you to look around and determine what your experience is through your five senses and through your internal processes?

A VERY "SENSE"ATIVE MAN

Even if you only get a surface-level sense of your external and internal processing of the moment you are sitting in right now, it will give you enough information to begin to understand how the subconscious mind becomes programmed.

programming from womb to 7

From the time a baby is in the womb, she takes in sensory learning that begins to prepare her for when she is born.

After her birth, the baby continues this process of learning with the addition of more inputs from the five senses. She doesn't know how to interpret these five senses. She doesn't know how to interpret experiences. She will rely on everybody around her to see what reactions and responses occur so she knows how to understand and interact in the world. At this point, she doesn't really have much in the way of thoughts, feelings, emotions, and beliefs. She hasn't learned that yet.

For a moment let's go back to our exercise that we did at the beginning of the chapter. If you looked around your environment and experienced it through your five senses and your thoughts, feelings, emotions, and beliefs, then you understand what it would be like to record that very moment in its fullest form. Imagine for this baby that every moment is being recorded in that much detail. In fact, imagine that for each of us we have this externally and internally full sensory picture for every moment from the womb until right now, and right now, and right now.

That is a lot of data!

This is an overly simplified version of the interaction of the human body and mind for purposes of understanding some basic relationships.

If the baby never did anything in life, she could be likened to a very advanced **camcorder** that is more like a **virtual reality suit** taking impressions of everything externally and internally for every moment. She has a photo album that she could step back into and experience each moment in full sensory detail. But since camcorders, however cool this one may be, can't even feed themselves, we as humans had to go beyond just being a recording device.

How old is yours?

She's six and a half weeks old but she's already learned how to record for 20 minutes at a time!

brain waves

Let's look at how the brain waves affect the storage of our experiences . . .

The brain has multiple levels of processing speeds that can be easily measured on an EEG machine. These varying speeds allow us to live and process our daily experiences and store and retrieve that information in different ways. These speeds are measured in cycles per second, known as hertz (Hz). The agreement on the actual speed of each range varies widely, but they are clearly defined by their characteristics.

Imagine you are taking a walk in the woods.

If you were practically standing still, you could "take in" every detail. If you started moving slowly, you would still take in detail, but have some less interaction between you and the woods. If you move into a little bit faster pace, still slow, you would be relaxed but not take in as much detail. Next, you would be in your normal daily routine mode, talking on your cell phone, and miss most of what was happening around you. Finally, you would move in a VERY high-pace mode and miss everything. These examples are like the categories of brain waves: Delta, Theta, Alpha, Beta, and Gamma.

Delta Waves 0.5–3 Hz

Delta is the slowest mode of brain waves. In this state, we can record everything that is happening around us in our subconscious mind. We are immersed in this state from the womb until 2 years old, so that we can take in all of the necessary instructions on how to live and navigate in the world.

After those formative years, we primarily have Delta waves in our deepest sleep state. So it's better to turn off those televisions while sleeping!

Theta Waves 4–7 Hz

Above Delta is the next higher level of waves called Theta waves. This is the primary state for a child between 2 and 7 years of age. For the rest of us, this usually occurs when we are just going to sleep, during REM sleep, just waking up, or deep in meditation. This is a hypnotic state that allows for high levels of storage and retrieval in the subconscious mind. It is more accessible than Delta for most people, therefore very useful for understanding and working with our unconscious patterns.

Alpha Waves 8–13 Hz

Alpha is the next level, with waves that create a very relaxed and awake state. This resting state for the brain is a platform from which we can access information that is below normal consciousness.

This is exemplified by the occasional "brilliant" ideas we have when waking up. Theta waves help us to retrieve the stroke of genius from our unconscious mind, while Alpha waves help us to make the idea conscious as we write it down.

Beta Waves 14 to 30 Hz

Beta waves are found in our normal, fully awake state. Higher Beta waves can feel more stressful. Lower Beta waves are associated with clarity and attention when we are very comfortably awake and productive.

Above Beta is the Gamma state. The Gamma level has very fast waves and can facilitate states of conscious aware-ness that are associated with the highest levels of creating and flow.

THE LEADERSHIP LAB

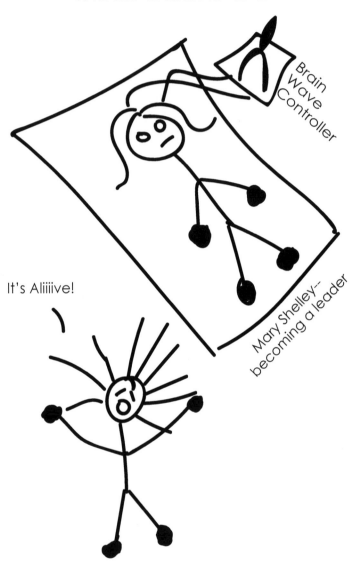

bringing
brain waves together

If we were to paint a picture using the three primary colors separately, it would be a very simple piece of art. But by combining colors, we create a more complex painting. Similarly, more than one brain wave type is present at any given moment. As leaders, we can practice using and combining the various brain waves to achieve a desired experience in the world. Theta waves can be combined with Gamma waves to produce peak performance experiences of creativity and effectiveness. Inducing Alpha and Theta waves can create an environment to write and retrieve information in the subconscious mind.

brain waves
and life experiences

As we have seen, from the womb until about 7 years of age, we have a predominance of Delta brain waves moving into Theta waves. During the Delta wave predominance, we are a pure sponge soaking up what we see in language, reactions, and behaviors. As we saw earlier, we continue to "take pictures" of our experience of everything going on around us. During this process, we strongly adopt the language patterns and beliefs of the people in our environment.

The Visionary Zone . . .

. . . inside of the bubble, imagine what resources you have that could help you move your vision into your reality.

During the latter part of this critical programming period, the child is in Theta wave predominance. She takes in most of what is said and done around her, but may add more of her own meaning and decisions about the circumstances. These decisions will come to form her beliefs that sit alongside her caregivers' beliefs. These are now programmed beliefs in her mind and nervous system. Throughout her life, her decisions will filter through these beliefs and change both how she perceives and interacts with the world.

Before the age of 3, she doesn't look at herself as a separate individual, but more as a part of everything going on around her. At around the age of 3, she begins to take on a more individuated identity. At around age 6 or 7, she moves into higher brain wave states like Alpha and Beta. The result is a formed "person" who has most of her programming that will support her to live in this world.

What if . . .

What would happen if 95 to 99% of our process was conscious and the rest was unconscious?

Generally speaking, our parents did their best based on the programming that occurred for them when they were younger, which was based on their parents' programming, and so on. This is why many patterns, good and bad, can be passed through generations.

Often this brings up feelings of unfairness that we didn't really have a say in our programming. This series is designed to help leaders uncover the programming that gets in the way of creating. Who knows, you may even stop patterns that have been going on for generations!

JOE'S GARAGE

three types
of programming

1. The moment-by-moment recordings of our experiences in full-sensory detail. This represents our **education** in this world that helps us to navigate new experiences.

2. The decisions, known as **beliefs**, that we made or we adopted from our parents about the experiences we have had in life. These are stored with our experiences.

3. The mechanism that amplifies recordings of **peak** or **traumatic** experiences in a way that is easily retrieved later by the nervous system.

When a child begins to grow up, those three types of stored programming will help her to know where to go and what to do to stay safe and to experience the life that she will experience. She will still learn. But that learning will take more effort and certainly not come at the intense speed that allows a child to pick up 3 or 4 languages concurrently while learning to walk, eat, negotiate human relationships, and get all of her needs met.

After 6 or 7 years of age, she will have to find ways to make use of slower brain waves, changes in life, new learning experiences that heighten her awareness to survive, or physical and mental exercises. Each of these are possibilities for fostering her creativity to help her become more of a leader.

recording
in the mind complex

We have seen how each moment is recorded for us in its fullest sensory detail based on how it was when we were there in that moment.

Could you pull up your experience from earlier when you looked around the environment?

See if you can recall a time when you were very happy in a nature situation. It could be a hike in the woods, a walk on the beach, or whatever you choose.

In your picture, you may get a sense of the experience. Some of the senses will be more clear than others. But try to allow more of the 5 senses from this experience to come in. What did you hear, see, smell, taste, and feel on your skin? What internal thoughts were you having, if any? What feelings and emotions were there?

This recall is what happens anytime we are with an old friend and we start remembering when . . .

In those circumstances we often pull up what seems like a two-dimensional version of the recording. But if we put more focus on it, we can recall more of our sensory experience of that moment.

Because we have recall, we can understand how programming works in the first place. Now let's see what it looks like when our subconscious recall seems to go wrong. If you are relaxed and look around you, your recording will happen with normal sensory input. If you had a heightened moment where you were overly excited or overwhelmed, your hormones and neurotransmitters will influence your sensory perception. Because of the change in your perception, the recording will be more vibrant or distinct from the other recordings.

In his brain and mind . . .

For example, let's say that in the above exercise, I recalled a time when I was walking on the beach. I remember the sunset was absolutely gorgeous, and the waves were crashing in such a way that I was having a peak experience of being connected to nature.

This releases hormones and neurotransmitters that heighten my sensory perception. This picture is stored with those heightened senses, including the brilliance of the colors, the smell of the ocean, and the deeply connected feeling that I had.

As another example, let's say that on my way home, I lost my wallet and would have to travel 200 miles without money. As a result, I feel *very, very* unsafe about the circumstance. On this negative end of the spectrum, just as with the positive example of the sunset, there will be an increase in the sensory perception of colors, shapes, people, sounds, emotions, and so forth that are recorded.

Most other recordings of our life experiences that come in between the heightened experiences have much less intensity of sensory perception when they happened and were recorded.

retrieval of memories

Sometimes our retrieval of memories is done voluntarily, as in recalling a memory from a wedding or information that supports a task of our job.

Sometimes memories are recalled but do not come into conscious view in that same way. This is because there is a safety system that is in place that is supported by the two parts of the brain called the amygdalae.

The amygdalae "look" at every detail of the stored heightened pictures. They compare the current environment to the recorded contents of these heightened experiences looking for a match in any detail. If the detail reflected in a recorded negative experience is a match to a detail in our current environment, then the amygdalae signal the body to engage in a "fight or flight" response to avoid the situation.

This would be similar to how we process information when we are in person as opposed to looking at a photo. In person, we focus on the object of our attention. But when we have the advantage of a photo, we can access every detail in the picture. Similarly, when the amygdalae review a recorded memory, all of these details are accessible. The challenge with this is that the amygdalae have two blind spots in reviewing the heightened recorded experiences.

One disadvantage for the amygdalae is in the **missing context** that occurred in the original circumstance. My amygdalae may "see" a blue-eyed tall man in my current environment. Incorrectly, they match this to the man who broke my heart 20 years prior.

That is a *problem* because I like this new guy!!

Another disadvantage is in **relevance of details**. If I was 4 when my parents had a loud argument and decided to get a divorce, every detail around me is subject to being a culprit. The French fries that I was eating at that moment could be considered dangerous by the nervous system because of the amygdalae's inability to distinguish this as an irrelevant detail. I would have no idea that this occurred and created an allergy in my body at that moment.

Let's say my first-grade teacher yelled at me. The children were all laughing about it. The sun was shining through the window. A heightened-sense picture was very possibly stored in my subconscious. Along with that, I also recorded the decisions that I made, which can become beliefs, around that circumstance as well.

"I am stupid."

"Everybody hates me."

"I won't ever raise my hand again."

The amygdalae constantly survey my current environment ever since first grade. They make sure that nothing that resembles a teacher, a classroom laughing, the sun shining through the window, AND every other detail that was recorded in that moment is showing up right now. The amygdalae do not need to be correct about the assessment of this generalized threat, as false positives have kept our ancestors alive. It seems that the twitchy ones are where we came from. Those who weren't twitchy enough became dinner and not my lineage.

In most cases, the amygdalae's connection between the current environment and the first grade scene will be a false positive. If I hear a child's giggle, I may notice that I feel completely overwhelmed, as if I want to run away from the situation. But I feel I can't. None of this comes to me consciously, and I have no way of associating that overwhelming feeling back to the first grade trauma. And this is how recall can happen without consciously knowing it.

This can lead to a **generalization effect** in which the original scene is triggered over and over again. From there, everything in our current environment resembles a classroom, a teacher, or laughing students.

Taking into account the beliefs that were recorded at that time:

"I am stupid."

"Everybody hates me."

"I won't ever raise my hand again."

and you will likely find this person avoiding many things with no idea why that is happening.

This is **unconsciousness**.

This is the **barrier to creating**.

This is the **impediment**
to leadership.

This works the same way with peak experiences, such as the sunset or a great success. My amygdalae are looking for something that approximates those heightened recordings. That means I may find myself unable to keep a job while I am down at the beach as often as I possibly can be to relive the circumstance that I once had. This is one of many challenges that can lead to various addictions.

As we can see, a person who does not understand the unconscious mind lacks the freedom to do what they want to do or the ability to create what they want to create. Therefore, they can only be a leader to the level of the consciousness that they do have. For most people, that consciousness level is quite low. But the good news is that the areas we will explore help to improve that incredibly rapidly. Let's take a look into how some of that works.

the
central story

"Once upon a time . . ."

There was a typical family in a typical town who watched the typical television shows every week. John and Jane Doe were very happy to sit down with their two children, Jack and Jill, and enjoy the adventures of movies, have a laugh with the sitcoms, and cheer on their favorite reality stars.

One day, John and Jane decided to shake things up a bit, and they invited an exchange student, Peter, to stay with them. Peter lived in a remote village, but he was somewhat familiar with television. Some Westerners had brought a television to his village as a gift. They shared the responsibility of turning the television on and changing the channels.

The first night Peter stayed with the Doe family, he was a little more reserved and watched the program that was on, just as everybody else did. The second night, Peter got up and spoke harshly to the television set. The Doe family was bewildered and concerned for Peter, as his discontent with the reality star's plight was misdirected at the television set.

Jane spoke to Peter in a very nurturing tone, "What's wrong, Peter?"

Peter was startled that they didn't understand what he was doing. He said, "This is how we share our discontent with the shows we watch. This is how we change what is happening on a show, so it doesn't happen in the future!"

John asked Peter, "Do you know where this show comes from?"

And Peter said, "Comes from? What do you mean? It is *in* the television set."

John and Jane realized that Peter and his community falsely believed that the television was a box that contained all of the programming that it had. Since the Does lived in Los Angeles, they decided to take Peter and the family on a tour to see how television shows get *into* the television set.

They visited a major network studio, and the first stop was a live set with actors. Peter was amazed when he realized that shows he had watched "came from" here. But he couldn't understand how the actors projected *into* the television set. John brought him to a video camera and explained how it records its surroundings. John showed him how the recording could be transferred to DVD and played later on the television set. He explained that this program could also be sent directly to the set, all through something called broadcasting.

To show Peter how broadcasting works, they went to a "live" news broadcast. Peter was amazed that he could see the Anchor reading the news and also see him coming through the television set that was nearby.

Peter asked John, "How does that go through the air and get to the television set?!"

John responded, "I am not sure exactly what happens, but we will find someone to help us with that one."

When the news was over, John explained to Peter how the news was also recorded on a DVD and could be played again. When Peter saw the same news program on a recording, he began to understand that some broadcasts are live, and some broadcasts come from another time. And both are being broadcast through the air to television sets.

Peter was elated to know this information and couldn't wait to tell his village all about broadcasting. He didn't think they would believe him because it seemed so different from what they knew.

As they were coming to the end of the tour, they went to one final stop. A documentary was being filmed. The documentary was entitled, "The Body and Mind *are* the Television Set." The talent had just gone on break, and the director came to greet the Doe family. Jane, intrigued by the title of the documentary, asked what it was about.

The director, Nancy, said, "This documentary was designed to help its viewers understand the body and mind from a deeper perspective than our current education provides. This viewpoint could help people become healthier, happier, and create more of what they want for themselves and others in the world."

She went on to say, "If a Westerner gets sick *in* the body, most of us are educated to see the problem as something that went wrong *with* the body. This would be similar to assuming the television set is producing its own programming." Peter had a shy smile come across his face, recalling that he didn't understand this process before the tour.

Nancy continued, "We all record every moment in our lives in a format that is as real as the moment we experienced it. But what is rarely known is that we are **recording** that on something that is like a DVD. When we recall that later, it replays in our body and mind, like a television set."

Jack interjected, "So this is like a cool virtual reality suit with a recorder!" Everyone smiled at Jack's enthusiasm as Nancy laughed and nodded in agreement.

Nancy further illuminated the process. "When I *go back* to a memory and pull it up, I retrieve all of the sounds, smells, tastes, sights, external and internal feelings, thoughts and beliefs from the DVD-like storage place. They **replay** in my mind and my body, similar to how the television set replays a DVD.

"When we record our memories, there are two different types of recordings that affect how we 'press play,' and what happens when we do. One type of memory is simply a normal circumstance that we can recall — like reminiscing with an old friend or remembering how we perform an activity. The other type of memory results from the way recording works, and *this* is the one that gets many Westerners into trouble."

She continued, "When our memories are recorded in moments that are *really* exciting or *really* challenging, there will be extra intensity on these types of recordings that make it easier for our 'television' to get tuned into them. This can be a safety mechanism that helps humans to find the great things in life while avoiding the dangerous ones. But because we don't know this is happening, the mechanism has become faulty in our lives.

"This means each of us has a **live** broadcast within our body — to and from the world — while these special DVDs are trying to get through that same channel. This distorts the live broadcast, even as we are recording it. It is like we have a filter that changes what we are seeing in the world, without knowing that this has happened."

Jane spoke up, "Oh my! We have really gotten it wrong! This affects how I care for my children and our health and relationships and, well, everything!!"

Nancy smiled compassionately "Yes, Jane, it affects *every-thing*! In addition to that, if we don't realize how these 'DVDs' get recorded and how the 'play button' gets pressed on them, then they broadcast in the background much of the time, and we don't even know it. As a result, our lives do not represent what they could if we were simply in our live broadcast.

"An example of this could be when someone experiences shortness of breath in the body. Although Westerners grab for anything possible to explain this symptom, the knowledge is available for us to 'tune in' and find out what DVD was started. When we do, we may find that a situation has been recalled from the past when we were running away from someone. The experience of being out of breath was recording at that time, along with all of the details of the dangerous circumstance. The old circumstance could be triggered by something that is similar to the current environment. Perhaps the person was walking outside at night years later, which brought back the memory of being chased by a mugger, and that pressed the 'play' button for him. Now he is left looking for the "cause" of his breathing problem.

"This mechanism of how memories are stored and recalled is a very different way to understand how the body responds to our life experiences. It is far more empowering than to view the body as the 'television set that broadcasts on itself.'

"We all understand that the broadcast does not come from the television set. Because we can begin to understand this process, we can work to make the live broadcasts stronger, so the old broadcasts aren't replayed in a way that makes life less enjoyable and productive. We can also *go back* to the old broadcasts and re-record them in a way that makes them less of a problem, while we are trying to interact with our live broadcasts. Or, simply stated, what is *really* happening in the world around us.

"This documentary is designed to show how this process works, some ways to correct what may have become faulty, and methods that make sense beyond trying to fix the television set.

Again, we *know* it is the broadcast of the recording that is causing the difficulty."

John looked sheepish, as if he had the same limit in education about the workings of the body and mind that Peter had earlier about the television and its broadcast.

John said to Nancy, "I guess we all have a chance of going on live broadcast if we understand this process. Then we could choose to pull up the appropriate DVDs, as we consciously decide that we need the information!"

"That's right, John," Nancy said, while trying to cover the sigh. "I have only recently learned all of this myself, yet it makes every part of my life easier and more satisfying to know the rules of the game. If all we need to do is 'clear up' the old broadcasts that do come through, then we can find ourselves tuning into our live channel. This would best support us in navigating the world and our own lives. The result of that is endless possibility for creating an amazing society where everyone can tune in to the best live version of themselves and create from *that* place."

Peter began to fully understand the television *and* body-mind analogies and shared, "Grandfather teaches our village that when we are not feeling like ourselves, we need to go on a journey. That journey is sometimes into the woods or another place, but it is designed for us to 'go beyond' something that is inside of us. Is that how the broadcasting gets changed?"

To that, Nancy responded, "Yes, and much of our research has been a study of initiations and rituals in different cultures that change the perception, which is distorted by an old broadcast."

John asked, "Nancy, Peter raised a question earlier that may be related to this. How does the broadcast get to the television? How do we, as humans, send and receive broadcasts? And are *they* related?"

Nancy smiled, "These are really great questions. Let me at least address what I think may be happening with *our* broadcasts. Science recognizes that the space between us is not empty. Because there is *something* between us, I think it may contain fields that could store information that we can recall or project to others. If you have ever felt connected with someone, even half-way around the world, this becomes more understandable. This may begin to explain the mother's 6th sense, as well as where we are storing the information — *including* the faulty DVDs.

Jane quickly said, "Yes! Remember that time when Jack got hurt on the playground when he was with his friend's family. I *knew* something was wrong in that moment, which was confirmed when I called them to check in."

"Yes, Jane," said Nancy, "and it is common for mothers to have that radar out there.

"There are ways to access the information that was recorded with faulty recall. In many disciplines and traditions, these types of memories are stored as a disconnected part of ourselves that is said to 'hide' in our subconscious mind. We can rerecord a faulty DVD incident by tuning into it. By doing that, we can see what was overly heightened in the senses during the original recording, due to cortisol, adrenalin, and other hormones and neurotransmitters coursing through our bodies. When we do this in a calm state, it helps us to rerecord that situation as 'normal,' and the broadcast doesn't sit in our field looking for a similar problem to come along.

"A lack of understanding about this process reveals why a person who seems to have a dark cloud over her head can't seem to shake that problem. In some circles, the problem has been called 'the law of attraction,' while in others the solution has been called 'a path of enlightenment.' Some equate the path of understanding and addressing this phenomenon to cultivating a healthy psyche. No matter what it is called, when we understand this and do our own work, we become far more capable of creating what we want to create in life. AND we support others with their creations, rather than creating at the expense of others."

Jane said, "I can't wait until your documentary comes out. We will find out the specifics of how we can work with our 'live broadcasts' and make our family's and others' lives even better!"

Nancy proudly announced, "I will invite you to the Premiere, as these changes can make life better for all. This starts with an average family recognizing that there can be a better way to live life."

The Doe family and Peter left Nancy. Everybody was glowing with the new education that changed the way they interacted with the world, each other, and themselves.

That night, they turned off the television and simply enjoyed the "live broadcast" of each other's company.

We can see our lives differently —more beautifully— only when we take on a new perspective.

We continuously experience our environment around us as we filter it through our DVDs and project back into the world based on our old recordings.

There are *three ways* to improve our broadcast:

1. Tune into the "DVDs" and rerecord them, so they stop playing in the background

2. Tune into the live broadcast so fully that the DVDs stop playing

3. Upgrade the channel where we take in our broadcasts

Everybody has an individual formula for the path that will make the most significant improvements in leadership capabilities. And the above 3 paths *can* work together to increase our effectiveness as a leader. The 3rd category would significantly eliminate much of the unnecessary interference that happens in life. This is accomplished through a change in emotional states, thoughts, feelings, and beliefs. This can be done directly with tools that improve the internal senses. It *can* also be a byproduct of the first two upgrades.

Now let's explore further what created the "DVDs" and what is stored on them.

CHAPTER THREE

the 3 areas of unconsciousness

If I had a nickel for every
fully conscious thing
I had ever done...

I would still have a day job!

Programming in the mind and body complex is necessary, and without it, we would not function by ourselves for very long on Earth. The difficulty begins when our programming has some "bugs" that were created due to a lack of understanding how the subconscious mind works. That is complicated by the fact that few even know that we have unconscious programming AND unconsciousness about the bugs that are already there.

Our first job as a leader is to lead ourselves.

That becomes difficult when increased unconsciousness results in decreased **leadership** — decreased **power and ability to create**. This is why a downward spiral can create a further downward spiral. This is why bootstrapping is what it is, a very difficult and unleveraged experience of attempting improvement. And this job is absolutely impossible if we have no idea that these unconscious areas exist.

The process of writing a book is not always pretty . . . sticky notes and all!

Self-portrait

Because I was so unconscious of this process throughout my life, it took 48 years for me to become aware of the specific challenges of unconsciousness. Because of my painstaking experience during this process, I can bring what I have learned to you in a relatively simple format. Maybe you can save the half century of suffering, the thousands and thousands of hours of research, and make it simpler to walk a more direct path to improved leadership.

In order to lead, we need to understand the types of unconsciousness, and ultimately, what we can do with them. We have already introduced each of these areas in the previous chapter. Here we will define them more clearly and dig into them to see how the programming **bugs** in each area can deplete our power to create.

1. education
and experiences

As we have noted, we are recording experiences in every moment of our lives. But because education has become synonymous with school, many people don't consider that all of these moment-to-moment recorded experiences, including classroom instruction, comprise our education.

In this way, the concept of education is redefined.

Imagine if you lived in a cave for your first 30 years and never saw another human. Your experience of the world would be devoid of written or spoken language, culture, technological advances, manners, relationships, pens and pencils, toothpaste . . . you get the point. There would be a complete barrier between you and the world in which you live. These missing educational experiences would act as a programming bug, diminishing your ability to interact with life due to your lack of education.

Missing education is significant only to the level that our interaction with the world becomes impeded. A person could get along well in his livelihood, relationships, and personal well-being with little to no formal education, as long as he has enough experiences to function well in his environment. This happens in many parts of the world right now.

Missing education becomes a bug when our experiences, which are our education, prove inadequate to navigate the circumstances in which we find ourselves.

Every culture, including the Western culture, holds the norms or beliefs that indicate the way that we must behave to be included in that society. If someone finds themselves outside of that cultural norm, they will often suffer in some form. We have to have a way to learn these norms in order to operate well in our "chosen" society. When our formal and informal education misses out on these rules, then we aren't interacting with life in the same way as others who are upholding these norms. Thus, we struggle in all areas of our lives to the level that we are missing education.

Much of this education on a cultural level is done without inspection, without consciousness. Many of the beliefs of those who came before us unconsciously become the norm for how we do things. This makes sense since we understand now how the programming happens from womb to six or seven years of age. Generation to generation, there is a passing down of the behaviors of the family and the greater society.

When I was a boy...

REALLY, Dad!?!

We recognize this experience of being outside of societal norms when we find ourselves in an unfamiliar situation. Everyone, likely, has their own experience of this. It may be finding ourselves sitting at a table not knowing what spoon to use OR not understanding the casual communication rules of a group with which we are engaged. Either way, you recognize through the ridicule of a smirk or the subtle hints of exile that there is an unwelcoming experience in which you are involved. This can often keep people locked into a very narrowly defined **comfort zone** that resembles our upbringing.

There is a term used in British cultures that addresses when one attempts and achieves a betterment in life. This term is called the "Tall Poppy" syndrome. When a poppy grows taller than the rest of the field, it gets cut off.

Ouch!

This term is used in two very different ways.

In one interpretation, it is used to help society. Sometimes when a person achieves an accomplishment, he may begin to act like he is better than others. The use of the expression is intended to help ground that person in order for him to find his humanity.

Occasionally, the term is misinterpreted and then misused to "cut off" a humane and grounded person, simply because he has achieved an accomplishment.

This latter use could *kill* a society!!!

The second use creates an entire cultural infrastructure to ensure that every leader feels incredibly uncomfortable at best, or is incapacitated at worst. When we speak of leadership and creating, we are talking about going beyond what is already created. Therefore, support is necessary in any process that requires us to move beyond what has traditionally been our comfort zone. In order to do that, we can follow the first interpretation of the term to support the humanity and grounded-ness of each leader as he creates. A culture that supports experiences and a more complete education in these leadership skills will foster a society that is more sustainable, more satisfying, and more creative.

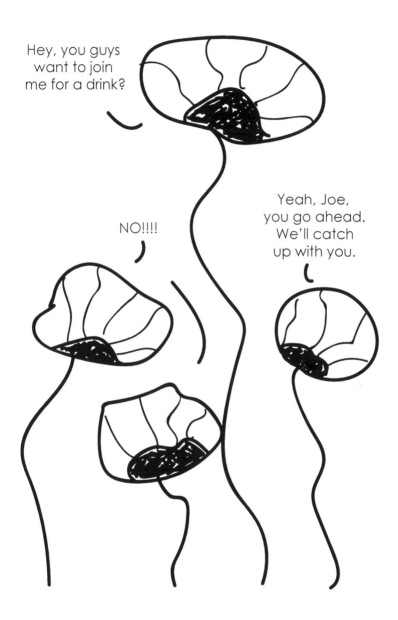

POPPY FIELD POLITICS

As much as missing education seems fairly benign, it is a very significant condition of unconsciousness and should be taken seriously. In order to acquire the missing or necessary education and experiences, it is important that we note the difficult places in our work, relationships, interests, and daily interactions in life. Once we see where we are struggling, we can create our own curriculum to close the gap and come to full competence. Missing education can make us more vulnerable. It can set us up to create other unconscious programming bugs, namely **beliefs,** that limit our experience of the world and our lives.

2. limiting beliefs

Let's assume that we have an excellent **education** that supports a comfortable interaction with every experience we will ever have in the world.

Let's add on top of that a **belief** system that is ACCEPTING of every experience we would ever have without imposing our own limiting judgements, meanings, or stories about those experiences.

If this could be reality, there would be no limits to what we can create.

We would be simply limitless.

Imagine the lives of Joe and Mark if they held these wildly different beliefs.

Joe:
"The world is a completely dangerous place and tries to harm me at every opportunity."

Mark:
"I accept that every single experience in life has been designed for my betterment, and I can handle anything that happens."

These extreme examples are designed to illustrate how these beliefs can affect the lives of Joe and Mark.

Joe's belief would alter his experience of the world by distorting his senses. His eyes and ears will be more attuned to danger, missing the subtle visual and musical treasures that make life pleasurable. In the extreme, nearsightedness replaces healthy vision, as his eyes attempt to protect him by "blocking out" some of the danger. His digestion could be compromised when the nervous system diverts blood flow to the limbs because his fight or flight response is often triggered. The negative experiences reinforce his limiting belief and create new ones, like his boss is difficult, he'll never find a girlfriend, and on and on. And Joe has no conscious idea of what is going on. He just sees this as normal.

Mark, on the other hand, holds a belief that makes it virtually impossible to create other limiting beliefs. Because he has a nervous system that seems relatively free of these limits, he doesn't take on new ones. He has the potential to create powerfully without even having to do any work on his areas of unconscious programming.

Mark doesn't exist. He couldn't. Even if you found one parent who was so perfect at parenting—and you can't—then you would never find a second who was as well. And they would never find each other to get together to make this non-existent Mark.

There are many Joes in this world and we are all, in some ways, experiencing life the way that Joe does. The belief may change and your senses may have reacted differently from his, but your power is still diminished by what you don't know . . . yet!

Every person sees the
world differently.

Imagine that a belief is like a pair of glasses with distorted lenses. Those lenses change the way the world appears to us. A programmed belief as simple as "I don't like men" or "I don't like women" would change all of our experiences in how we relate to half of the population.

Part of the challenge is that glasses, *beliefs*, diminish our interaction with and experience of life. The belief in our example may alter the person's experience of life by as much as 90 to 99%, as the opposite sex is found in far more than half of life's circumstances. That person will likely find himself avoiding or not fully interacting with many situations. His level of effectiveness as a leader could also be diminished by a large percentage.

And this is one belief!!

Cindy,
what's going
on with Tom?!!

Oh, that!
The doctor did a bunch
of tests and determined
he is severly low on his
acceptance of reality as
well as deficient in his
appreciation levels.
He'll recover!

GRRRR!

We all have many, many, many pairs of glasses that change the way that the world is viewed. That, in turn, changes how we interact with the world. Beliefs represent a hardwired and programmed version of what we are willing to accept, and more importantly, what we are not willing to accept. *Life happens.* If our beliefs are programmed in a way that doesn't allow us to comfortably accept life's experiences, we will find ourselves in anxiety and stress about life. We won't know that this was an unconsciously programmed bug that created a problem. Yet, just as the invisible force of electricity can harm us when we don't understand its laws, a limiting belief can also damage our lives and stifle creativity.

When our educational limits leave us vulnerable and our limiting beliefs make our comfort zone smaller than our daily challenges, we are far more exposed to a type of overwhelm that has a very specific effect on our nervous system. These types of experiences are called traumas.

We all have them.

Some are larger, some smaller. Because of the cumulative difficulty that they create for us, let's look at how traumas work.

3. overwhelming experiences (traumas)

When we are unable to accept a situation as it is based on our programmed limits of education and beliefs, our first line of defense is to fight or to flee. This would likely keep the nervous system fairly healthy without any newly programmed limits. When we are in a situation with a perceived level of threat to our survival or well-being, with no option to fight or to flee, the nervous system becomes frozen in that moment.

To illuminate the freeze response, it is imperative to understand what is supposed to happen in our nervous system. A wild animal can experience an overwhelming sense of fear in its nervous system. Imagine a coyote is chasing a rabbit. The rabbit's nervous system could cause him to freeze during this chase, in which case he would stop moving. A few things can happen from this. First, the rabbit may not be spotted since many predators are attracted by movement. Second, the rabbit would have produced enough protective chemicals to ensure that it wouldn't feel the full pain of being eaten if that becomes the eventuality. Third, the coyote may have been drawn to the chase, but seeing the frozen rabbit, he is no longer interested.

When the chemistry that caused the freeze in the rabbit's nervous system wears off, the rabbit may begin to shake uncontrollably. Upon closer inspection, it is noted to be a fast action version of the steps that the rabbit couldn't complete when the freeze occurred.

Because the rabbit is able to complete these steps and clear the short term memory, the rabbit does not store this trauma in its nervous system. This is the way that all wild animals are capable of keeping their nervous systems clear of traumas.

As I said, all wild animals do this. Domesticated — caged — animals don't. That is why we see pets becoming traumatized. Little dogs begin to shake, so they can process the fear that is moving through their nervous system. We immediately reach down to pick them up and hold them so they can't shake. Trauma.

They are yelled at for doing something that they don't understand and then trained to behave a certain way that leaves no room for dissipating the energy. Trauma.

We train dogs to be good without taking into account the senses they have that alert them to danger — such as fear of a neighbor. They know often long before we realize the neighbor was, indeed, a danger. And as we yell at the dog for barking and acting nervous around the neighbor, the dog just logged another trauma in the nervous system.

Perhaps it's less obvious that humans are also caged or domesticated via the beliefs that are held in place by society. Those beliefs represent the norm that we haven't lived up to that made life dangerous for us. This was seen in the example of a first grade version of me being yelled at by the teacher and laughed at by the students.

Relatively few of us are physically threatened by wild animals, as our ancestors were. But we have threats to our survival that occur because of our social norms.

In the recent past, not living up to the social norms could mean exile from the village. If you were exiled from society at that time, you were so vulnerable that death was a very high possibility.

On a very deep level, humans feel the threat of being exiled any time that they don't fit in to the social norm. And there are ways of creating exile that we employ in our current day. (Tall Poppy).

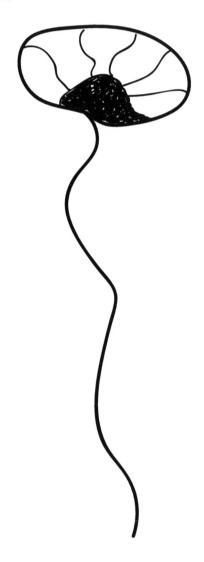

What must be present in order to experience a trauma? There must be a feeling that there is no escape, no fighting or fleeing is possible. Along with that, it has to be a threat to our survival on some level. We will usually perceive that we are isolated in that moment. The educational deficits, limiting beliefs, and older traumas that are already unconsciously programmed feed into our assessment of the threat of our current situation. But once a person has gotten to a place where the freeze response is activated, the nervous system marks that experience.

When the trauma occurs, our nervous system lowers our consciousness, and we record the incident in a subconscious container. This can be called different names in different circles. In psychology, it creates an inner child or contributes to our shadow selves. In indigenous cultures, it can be called a soul part. In each of these cases, it is considered a part of us that "breaks off," protecting us from the brunt of the trauma in that moment.

This becomes further complicated when the nervous system records the traumatic incident. The body increases specific hormones and neurotransmitters that sharpen our senses in order to bring us to safety. That increase in sensory awareness is stored in the recording of this traumatic incident as vibrant colors, sounds, and so forth. The incident is tagged in our nervous system as something to avoid. The amygdalae will assess the current environment for anything that approximates a detail of this traumatic scene. That means that we are constantly filtering our current life experiences through this new trauma.

Remember, the amygdalae are there to keep us safe, not happy.

Understanding this process is critical for when we resolve the energy that is stored as a trauma. Humans are domesticated by our cultural norms, which create the "cage" in which we live. These norms also keep us from dispelling the energy that accumulates in the nervous system when we have found ourselves to be frozen.

In addition to recording our external and internal experience of a trauma, the nervous system records the new beliefs that we create in that moment — and we always do. Therefore, we have a traumatic experience that is as current to the amygdalae as when it happened, AND we have new beliefs that shape how we look at everything in our current environment.

In working with traumas, it is common to find that people change their trajectory in life. After being embarrassed at a party, they could vow to "never go to a party again." This creates an entire life that is built around this new belief. All, of course, unconscious to the person involved.

Isn't it amazing that this whole unconscious world is operating for you and for everyone else, mostly unknown to all of us, but it affects every minute of the day!?!

I would say this is a major gaping hole in our educational system. This is quite a bit more important to our successful interaction in life than learning about the capital of a place that I can't even pronounce.

Kudos to *you* for filling this gap for yourself.

the flow
of unconsciousness

If we were never exposed to any of the bugs of the 3 areas of unconsciousness, we *could* live a life without them. This occurs because an education that created 100% comfort in every circumstance would keep us from ever creating a limiting belief. A pervasive belief that created acceptance for everything that ever happens to us, would make it impossible for a trauma to occur.

And here's the kicker: having only the single belief that says, "I accept EVERYTHING exactly as it is," which filters how we experience life, would keep all traumas away. It would also make missing education a non-issue.

This does not purport that we should retreat from experiencing life fully, but it shows how we can adjust our beliefs and experiences to support our power and ability to create.

Conversely, unconsciousness stacks on itself. We know this as the downward spiral. When we do have missing education, it can create limiting beliefs, which can create traumas. Then the traumas can create more limiting beliefs which can blind us to or make us avoid the necessary educational experiences in order to be fully engaged in life.

A simple example of this is when we attend a wedding from another culture. If the rituals are unfamiliar, we can create a belief that, "this is strange." That will be reinforced and pick up evidence throughout the ceremony. Finally, when the bottles are being broken and the chairs are flying overhead, voila! We just logged a trauma. Then we see that co-worker at work on Monday morning and start to feel nervous for some unknown reason. After avoiding them and everyone like them, we watch our world get smaller and smaller . . . and don't know why.

A **bucket** can be used to symbolize the 3 areas of unconsciousness. If we have a bucket that fills up with every recording from each moment of our lives, we can imagine this to be like a sequentially-timed photo album. This represents the totality of our educational experiences in life. In between the "pictures" are the decisions we made that, in some cases, are hindering us now. These are the limiting beliefs. And within the photos, we find the peak and traumatic experiences are more vibrantly recorded for quick view, so the amygdalae can continue to filter the environment through them to keep us safe.

These are the traumatic experiences we avoid and the peak experiences we are attached to, both unconscious.

This bucket is ours to carry.

This bucket is the work of our lifetime.

This bucket is us, as individuals,
our "ego," our character.

This bucket is what supports
our great moments.

This bucket is what creates our shortcomings.

This bucket limits our power to create.

This bucket limits us as leaders.

This bucket can be transformed.

Unconsciousness can be transformed.

The **comfort zone** we have is unconscious to us until we understand what is in our bucket. If our bucket is very limited, our lives will have to be limited to maintain a sense of comfort.

The larger we make our bucket, through more diverse experiences *without bugs,* the more our comfort zone will encompass. Our bucket creates the limits in the scope through which we experience our lives. Whatever the scope encompasses is contained within our comfort zone. What goes outside of the scope is part of our **(dis)comfort zone**. If we want to increase our power to create as leaders, we need to become comfortable with going further into our (dis)comfort zone.

Everything in our bucket was created at a time when each experience, belief, and trauma required that response for our greatest level of survival *in that moment.* If I was mugged in a park and unconsciously decided that parks are a dangerous place, *that* made sense for that circumstance, but not for *every* circumstance after that. Now, when I walk past a park and become fearful, it is inappropriate to this circumstance, barring any true danger. This is **projection**. And it is worst when we don't know the unconscious elements that are making it happen. Projection is about recalling peak and traumatic experiences and beliefs unconsciously and super-imposing them on the present moment.

We are constantly projecting old experiences that are unconscious to us into the present environment. Our job as leaders is to recognize that we have unconsciousness in the form of a bucket. It is also our job to resolve the bugs found within, producing more consciousness. When we do that to the greatest extent, we become *limitless* creators of a very healthy environment in the world that surrounds us.

When we work with our bucket step-by-step, we project less, lead more, and leave space for those around us to achieve their greatest levels of leadership.

Note: In society, many have a negative reaction to the word "consciousness." As we can see from the first 3 chapters of this book, it is imperative to understand consciousness and unconsciousness in order to function responsibly and effectively. If we recognize that a word feels negative to us but we know it can be positive and supportive, we can acknowledge that a limiting belief may be operating below our consciousness. We don't *have* to know the origin that creates this negative reaction. But we can reap the benefits of willfully changing our response to a word in order to better support ourselves.

resolving unconsciousness

We have already noted in the education section that when we come across a place of missing education, we can create our own curriculum to close the gap.

The limiting beliefs and the traumas take a little bit more of an in-depth study. I have found amazing tools for changing the recordings, beliefs, and traumas which I will share later. I am devoting the second book to diving much deeper into these areas of unconsciousness because of how critical they are to one's ability to create. But I would be remiss if I didn't share with you *some* tools that have helped me.

It seems like all of these internal and external senses come so easy to you. Do you have a special sense that we don't know about, like a 6th <u>sense</u>?!

Ah, maybe. My recording device came with a built-in <u>sense</u> of humor. But anyone can pick up that accessory if their model didn't come with one!

As for handling limiting beliefs, one of the easiest ways to determine if they exist is to set out to accomplish a vision or a goal.

As you begin to take the steps toward attaining the vision or goal, be very conscious of places where you find it difficult or impossible to perform these steps. A question like, "What might I believe about _____," can begin to reveal the limits that are below your conscious awareness.

Let's use an example. One of my clients was uncomfortable with doing a specific marketing task for her own company.

This seemed odd to her because she had done this sort of task with many clients. She recognized that her belief was holding her back. In order to find the limiting belief, she asked herself, "what might I believe about advertising this service?" The answer came back that, "I shouldn't put myself out there." That is a problem for her, especially since every client interaction was a form of putting herself out there. That is when she recognized that she needed to understand the depth to which that belief impeded her progress.

If you find the unconscious limiting beliefs, you now have more ability to consciously override them in your daily life. Before we are conscious, we have no chance to expand. With consciousness, we can expand at will.

Now we understand the definition of Leadership, the unconscious mind, and the impediments to our power to create.

Next, let's take a look at a framework that can provide a path to our most limitless and powerful levels of creating

—The Leadership Score™.

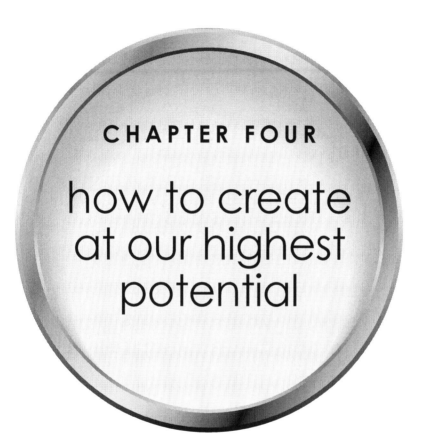

CHAPTER FOUR

how to create at our highest potential

When I am being my best me,
it feels nothing like me.

It's more like riding
a seriously powerful wave that is going
somewhere that I want to be!

As leaders, we have the power to create.

Leadership development is easier when we have a tool for measuring how effectively we execute that power and what gets in the way.

The Leadership Score IS that tool.

This framework is a guide to be "in the zone" constantly.

The first part of the Leadership Score introduces the scale of the *power to create.*

Deteriorating and weakening the ability to create is

−10 to 0

Creating and strengthening the ability to create is

0 to +10

The following graph illustrates this concept of the effectiveness of our leadership.

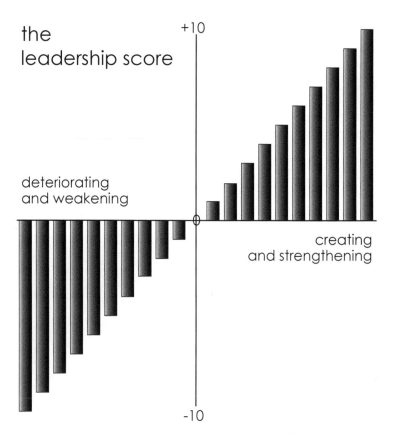

the
leadership score

+10

deteriorating
and weakening

0

creating
and strengthening

-10

As we are about to discover a detailed framework that out-
lines the nuances of our leadership and the measurements of
our creative power, let's see how the 3 areas of unconsciousness play a part in that score.

power to create

In our society, leadership is synonymous with competition. The current functional definition of competition would be something like "winning at the expense of others," without regard for our humanity. This was not always the case. In fact, the derivation of the word *competition* was from Latin and it meant "to seek together, to come together, to agree." We have strayed from that definition quite a bit.

A leader creates.

That's it, nothing more or less. Something doesn't exist, so a leader brings it into existence. And this means that everyone has the potential for leadership . . . **everyone**. If we simplify the definition of a leader, we can eliminate the impediments and improve the impact that we have. As part of this, we can re-examine the current concept of competition. That concept, in all its forms, is the killer of creativity, thus leadership.

The power to **create** can be blocked by the act of **competing**.

This is similar to the earth blocking out the sun, which impedes its light from reaching us at night.

The 3 areas of unconsciousness produce fear in our nervous system, blocking the power to create. This fear drives our perceived need to compete.

*Without the concept of creating,
there is no concept of leadership.*

*The definition of **create** is
to bring something into existence
that wasn't there.*

*The definition of **compete** is
to outdo, to take, to contend, to make less of.*

*When leaders work in the realm of
competing, they are comparing.*

This lowers their ability to see possibility.

This changes the nervous system.

"It seems too simple . . ."

Enter fear!

*Fear is the disease that gave life to the **zero-sum** game that we find so prevalent in society.*

*The wonderful news is that we can simply stop participating in such games and begin to **create**.*

When you limit yourself to competing, you are placing yourself in the fight-or-flight response as a result of the 3 areas of unconsciousness. This response limits the physical senses and the mind, greatly reducing your access to the possibilities that are available in your environment. Additionally, there is a cultural norm produced in media and advertising that creates a sense of "not being good enough."

These phenomena produce a fear that we will not meet our needs and desires. Culturally, we have responded to this perceived scarcity through an unhealthy cycle of competing to satisfy an unconscious standard.

The scale of the Leadership Score that determines our power to create was inspired in part by an idea from Wallace D. Wattles' 1910 book, *The Science of Getting Rich*. Wattles' idea is that the *competitive plane* is a place where your successes are achieved at the expense of others. He implies true power and wealth are not sustainable on this plane. He also suggests that the *creative plane* is a place that ensures that every vision and goal created and implemented would encompass betterment for all involved. ***This is sustainable leadership.***

Healthy competing is *inspiring* the best in yourself and others. The Williams sisters, who are world-class tennis players, are not trying to tear the other down when playing. They are trying to build themselves into the highest level of skill possible. If we maintained the original definition of compete — to seek together, to come together, to agree — it would be a form of leadership. But because the word has become synonymous with impeding the creation process, it represents a –10 "Leader."

Competition violates the Golden Rule, known in every culture in the world as something like, "Do unto others . . ." or "What you don't want done to you . . ."

This violation keeps us small and unable to create at the levels that are possible.

As soon as the Olympic athlete looks back at his competition instead of continuing to do his best in the race, he is often overtaken unnecessarily. We can instantly drop most of our own hindrances if we are able to focus on creating instead of competing.

Simply put, anything that is not fostering creating is strengthening the need to compete.

Now that we understand the need to process our 3 areas of unconsciousness in order to move from competing into creating, we can begin to unpack the 4 components of leadership that comprise the ability to create. The following graph is the main framework of the Leadership Score. The Power to Create is the overall measurement that is assessed on a scale of –10 Compete to +10 Create. Within that scale, there are 4 components — Visioning, Executing, Empowering, and Developing — which point us more directly toward the specific unconscious limitations in our power to create.

the leadership score

power to CREATE		visioning	executing	empowering	developing
+10	creating	all possibilities visible	effortless	inspiring	continuous
0	neutral	neutral	neutral	neutral	neutral
-10	competing	all obstacles visible	limited	discouraging	non-existent

visioning

The first tool of a leader that determines his power to create is how well he can envision something new, different, or better in any area of his life, business, or society. If he can do that well while existing in his present situation, he has a chance of realizing his vision.

FutureCam

A simple, yet powerful exercise in visioning would be to use a process that I call "FutureCam."

This process draws its power from the idea that we can release **all obstacles** found in our present external and internal environments and "go" to a specified time in the future where **all possibilities** exist.

FutureCam *can* even override some of the strongest limitations held in place by our 3 areas of unconsciousness and provide leverage to create more consciousness in those areas.

Finally, traumas *can* be a unique tool that provides a direct experience "in the future," fostering a far more powerful creation process. This will become clearer when we go into the methods for handling traumas in Stage 2.

What is a FutureCam?!

Let's return to the earlier exercise when we looked around our current environment. Through that, we discovered that all of the senses, external and internal, are being recorded in each and every moment of our lives.

We have seen how we experience life in this way through something of a virtual reality suit that records each of these moments.

Because we know how the virtual reality suit records in the present, and we can recall these full-sensory recordings of our experiences from the past, we can use this to "hack" the future to create a new reality.

The simple version of the FutureCam process is to determine the time period you want to "go to" — 3 months, 1 year, 3 years, or more. "Put on" your virtual reality recording device — fully embody your internal and external senses — and virtually go to that time.

Once you are in that timeframe, notice that the FutureCam virtual reality suit is specially equipped with sensing attachments.

YOU **decide** what you see, hear, feel, smell, taste, think, emote, sense, and believe. Change each of these senses *and* the physical environment to be exactly what you would like it to be. Remember, the suit only allows for *possibility visioning.*

There is no editor in this realm!

Often when I am with my clients, I will describe this visioning process as more of a story than a vision. This affords the client a sense of lightness that she can create whatever she wants right now, with the luxury of adjusting the story as needed.

This visioning process is not so much of a strict format as an opportunity to create clarity. This is a skill, like any other skill, and it takes some practice.

Which means in order to attain the skill, you would have to start practicing!

Life *can* feel random and confusing until we make a decision to clarify some aspect of our lives. Have you ever seen one of those booths where money blows around a contestant randomly? The contestant will remain stunned and ineffective at getting the dollars until she begins to focus on each single bill. For our visioning process, this means that the clarity of deciding on a vision eliminates all of the irrelevant obstacles and creates focus on the possibilities. We have to start by putting a stake in the ground in order to see if we have chosen the right place for the stake. Then we can adjust the vision based on that clarity.

Select your vision,
then adjust it until it works for you.

Two advantages come to the leader who clarifies a vision. He has and creates clarity for himself and those involved in the process, and he can harness the power of creation that is derived through attention and focus.

The Leadership Score is a diagnostic tool to determine if we are more focused on obstacles or possibilities.

When it is the former, we have just revealed more work to do in the 3 areas of unconsciousness.

And with the latter . . . create, create, create!

executing

If a leader clarifies his vision but cannot execute it, he will find his business failing, his family deprived, or his artistic endeavors left to die on the field of imagination.

Most of us have experienced a moment of being "in the zone" or "flow," a term coined by Mihaly Csikszentmihalyi. This state enjoyed by many, including athletes, artists, and spiritual seekers, transports them "beyond" themselves, simply flowing with the object of their focus. The state is associated with an exponential increase in productivity.

Many are interested in how to achieve this state on a more regular basis.

The scale of **limited** to **effortless** can be found in the Executing portion of the Leadership Score. Anything short of the effortless +10 level of realizing a vision reveals the internal work that can be addressed.

Don't know how to read an income statement? Learn it!

Have a limiting belief that says, "I can't?" Change it!

A step toward your vision retriggers a similar action that you were scolded for as a child? Process it!

And *execute* your power in creating limitlessly as a leader!

+10 Leadership IS the constant state of flow.

empowering

A leader is seldom on his own. If the leader is **discouraging** in his manner of interacting, then he is making less of those around him. If he is **inspiring**, then all will be better for having interacted with him. It is important that the empowerment component of leadership be developed to increase the impact that he can have with and through others.

I have taught extensively and do currently use a communication model for empowerment. A deeper study of the model and concepts will be available in the Empowering Chapter of the third and final book in this *Creating a Leader* series. But let's begin to look at a few principles here.

When we struggle with attention because we find ourselves in the fight-or-flight response, it is difficult, at best, to focus on the other person. This diminishes our rapport.

With low rapport, we don't recognize what is important to the other person. And that makes them less apt to recognize or care about what is important to us. Having skipped all of these steps, we make poor agreements based on assumptions which lack specificity and clarity. And when others aren't meeting our needs that even *we* aren't conscious of, we get frustrated.

This is where competition is born.

This is where we can get to work on becoming conscious!

This is where we become our most inspiring leadership selves.

developing

Developing is akin to adopting the attitude that we are always learning and improving through our interactions and experiences in life. Wielding the knowledge about the 3 areas of unconsciousness gives us a platform from which to improve our education, expand our beliefs, and heal our traumas, all in the name of creating more powerfully as a leader. Fun!

If you are not developing yourself, you are likely competing. As we have seen in the previous components, competition produces a discouraging, limited, obstacle-laden "leader." Not a choice anyone would make if they saw the reality of this!

There is great hope for this. Even, and maybe I should say especially, at +10 on **The Leadership Score**, leaders continue to develop themselves.

Why?

Because if they are creating at the highest level in their current sphere of influence, their sphere of influence will continue to expand.

Just think about what that could mean for your family, work, community, artistic endeavors, relationships . . .

+10 is like a first black belt.

The leader has mastered the basics, and now it is time to have some real fun with creating!

+10 leadership

When one finds their +10 leadership level of creating, life is more enjoyable, the time becomes more productive, the impact is far greater, and the power to create is limitless.

A leader who *visions*, *executes*, *empowers*, and *develops* at this level maintains the clarity and power offered by creating and executing a vision, while empowering all involved in the process.

And then she does it all again!

+10 Leadership is a choice to create more powerfully and responsibly.

This choice is available only when we realize that it is possible.

It IS possible!

+10 Leadership *is* Your Greatest You!

my vision, my hope

In my vision, every man, woman, and child has the *choice* to resolve the limiting programming that occurs from ages 0 to 7, creating fear and unconsciousness that gets projected out into the world and passed down generation to generation.

In that vision, those of us who choose to become conscious and use our courage to overcome fears can appreciate others without separating over differences.

In that vision, love is the main currency and language that is exchanged. Not a watered down, "I love you, but" type of love. A deep and profound source of creative power that allows us to create our own version of beauty in this world.

In that vision, conflicts are easily resolved because conflict is understood to be unconsciousness. We simply envision a new reality, devoid of conflict, and watch its beauty unfold.

In that vision, we innately understand free will, and we honor our own and others' realities and choices.

In that vision, we are each whole,
and we are all whole.

Join me for *Creating a Leader: Simply Powerful, Stage 2*. We will begin exploring the The Leadership Score in more depth. As we go deeper, we will uncover the entry points to greater leadership power. Creating will become second nature as we continue on this path.

See ya soon . . .

Proof

Made in the USA
Columbia, SC
27 June 2017